BOOGIE-WOOGIE CRISSCROSS

Tess Gallagher
&
Lawrence Matsuda

a plume editions book

AN IMPRINT OF MADHAT PRESS
ASHEVILLE, NORTH CAROLINA

MadHat Press
MadHat Incorporated
PO Box 8364, Asheville, NC 28814

The Library of Congress has assigned
this edition a Control Number of
2016903908

ISBN
978-1-941196-29-8 (paperback)

Text by Tess Gallagher and Lawrence Matsuda
Cover art by Matt Sasaki
Cover design by Marc Vincenz

Plume Editions
an imprint of MadHat Press
www.MadHat-Press.com

First Printing

BOOGIE-WOOGIE CRISSCROSS

Dedication

LAWRENCE

This book is dedicated to my late parents who were born in America and incarcerated in Idaho during WWII based on their race, my wife Karen, my son Matthew, his wife Jesika, and my Hiroshima relatives who survived the atomic blast.

TESS

to Josie Gray, Jade Gray, Karen Gray, Lee Gray and Gemma Gray, Brian Questa, Hiromi Hashimoto, Alejandro Inarritu, Savita Halappanavar and Dhara.

Contents

Introduction   xi

I. *Pow! Pow! Shalazam*

The poets regarding Pow! Pow! Shalazam   3

Kisses   5

What They Missed   7

Fifteen Love, the Bloop-Shot Return   9

A Dervish of Kisses   10

Even Gangsters Need "R"s   12

When Cars Were Bedrooms   14

Wisp of a Gal   16

Epona Meets X-Men   18

Starlings   20

II. *Blue Cocoon*

Some thoughts from the poets regarding Blue Cocoon   27

Rose City Vacation   29

Cat Mountain   32

Cat Island and Bunny Town   35

By the Sea   38

Island within an Island   40

III. *Wild-Haired-Labyrinth Renga*

Some thoughts from the poets regarding Wild-Haired
  Labyrinth Renga   45

Careening Toward Forever-after   47

Dear Cloud, Dear Larry   50

Old Mick's Wisdom   54

Button, Button   57

Holy Fig   62

The Paper Airplane of Justice   65

Ghost Dahlias   68

If Your Brother's Wings Are Melting   71

In Memory of Kip   74

Acknowledgments   77

Art Credits   79

About Tess   81

About Larry   83

Introduction

In the late summer of 2011 Tess Gallagher and Lawrence Matsuda were e-mailing each other while she was in her cottage in the west of Ireland and he was at home in Seattle. The exchanges evolved into a series of nine poems. The collaboration was like a poetry jam session where they traded and borrowed images, ran riffs on each other's poems in a responsive, competitive, and lighthearted way.

The resulting initial section entitled *Pow! Pow! Shalazam!* was published in the April 2013, Issue #22 of *Plume Poetry*. In 2014–15, two additional collaborative segments evolved: *Wild-Haired-Labyrinth Renga* (nine poems) published in *Plume,* and *Blue Cocoon* (five poems) was finished in August of 2015 for publication in *Plume's* April 2016 edition. The three sections consisting of 23 poems and artwork were then combined to create *Boogie-Woogie Crisscross* in Fall 2015.

At the start of each section they have given some thought as to what was happening in their exchanges. Early on, Tess characterizes the style as being "kind of hip and comic book and jangly," and also "prickly with antennae." Like any dance it's also an invitation to lose time and as Larry says—to show your "chops." A kind of dueling banjos.

Tess Gallagher
Co. Sligo, Ireland

Larry Matsuda
Seattle, Washington

Fall 2015

xi

American vs. American (detail), Roger Shimomura

POW! POW! SHALAZAM
Section I—Summer of 2011

The poets regarding *Pow! Pow! Shalazam*

LARRY MATSUDA:

Since e-mails are fragile, it occurred to me that twenty years from now no one would discover Tess's and my correspondence tucked away in a dusty attic. After finding her book *Portable Kisses* at Elliot Bay Books, I thought I would be a wise guy and challenge her to a poetic duel as a way to preserve some of our e-mails. I sent her "Kisses" and her response was like a tennis slam. I was stunned and responded with humor since something serious would have surely been deadly. That reply begat another response and another. The exchange was like a karate pupil challenging the master—like Daniel and Mr. Miyagi from *The Karate Kid*. I wondered, "As a challenger, did I have the chops to go five rounds with Tess, the champion?"

TESS GALLAGHER:

I have always been fascinated by reciprocity—that is, the way one thing happens and then responsiveness gets going that would never have occurred without that initial stimulation. Larry is responsible for getting things going. Without really proposing an exchange, he presented a very tasty poem that was invitation enough. I suddenly seemed only able to speak back to him in "poem."

Writing toward Larry's poems was not like writing to Larry. It was beyond Larry. Although I know many things Larry likes—such as Marilyn Monroe and salmon fishing—I also seemed to be trolling for things I didn't know about him. We both love salmon fishing and I go with my brother, Tom, each summer and fall to catch silvers & kings for my winter food from the Strait of Juan de Fuca.

I hadn't fully realized, however, Larry's love of comics, but the poems discovered that. Anyhow, there was a snap, crackle and pop to these exchanges. When writing toward Larry, I felt faster and smarter than I know myself to be.

About Larry and me—we became friends through a mutual friend, the Seattle painter Alfredo Arreguin, whom I've known for fifty-five years. I was visiting Alfredo when he handed me a manuscript Larry had left for him to show me. It was all about Minidoka, the Idaho internment camp finally starting to be recognized for what it was—a concentration camp for Japanese American citizens and Japanese immigrants during WWII.

The poems recounted the ways in which Larry's birth inside the camp had affected him. It also detailed the impact on his family and other Japanese Americans. I was so moved by these poems that I physically could not get up from the table. Alfredo kept passing me in the room and saying: "That's okay, Tess. You don't have to read every poem. Just read a few so I can tell Larry you looked at it." So our relationship actually began in paralysis of attention—poems that made me unable to put them down. Eventually this manuscript became *A Cold Wind from Idaho*, published by Black Lawrence Press.

I thought of what we did in our exchange, which happened from Seattle to Ireland and back (I was in my cottage in Co. Sligo), as more freeing and playful, giddy even. We were like a brother and sister playing tag or daring each other. In any case, I loved every morning getting up and finding a new poem from Larry on my computer and composing right onto the computer, which I never do.

Larry caused this velocity, since you just wanted to answer him as quickly as possible, despite the eight-hour time difference. Because I was on the computer, I started looking for information about Marilyn Monroe that might delight him, and also scouting up details about cars, for which there is really a lot of lovely screwball language.

The poems compounded like a snow-woman, aggregations of crystals and meltdowns, freeze-ups and slump-offs. They felt kind of hip and comic book and jangly, but also prickly with antennae, open to so much that I hadn't known might be there. Mainly, I'd say it was really a lot of fun. Poetry can get so serious, plodding around about death and lost love and failed this and that. Maybe what this sequence says is: "Go out and play!"

Summer 2011

(The Challenge from Larry to Tess)

KISSES

for Tess after finding her book *Portable Kisses*

Between "F" and "H"
at Elliot Bay Books
I discover your
57 poems about kisses.

Were you on the book cover
in a 1955 Ford convertible
locked in a front-seat embrace?
For an instant I become a voyeur—

woman thrown back
in his arms,
skirt hiked up
where little buttons
snap elastic to nylons.

Half-eaten popcorn bag askew
between the couple in
an American drive-in theatre,
stock image your editor picked?

The photo is the click-click
of dial phones, whacking
typewriter keys,
scent of goopy white-out,
and spinning vinyl LPs—
drive-in theatres with squirming lovers
in convertibles populate
American elephant graveyards.

Did the universe feel the void
of kisses as each screen
was devoured by tractors,
like fields of stars banished
from a torn-down sky?

(Response from Tess)

WHAT THEY MISSED

was not the movie flickering
across rabbits and night-incubating
golf balls flown in from the course nearby, but
Time's inter-splicing of trespass, ennobling
the shortcomings of clothing as a dampening
effect on teenage ardor. What were they
thinking of, parents, to allow that side-door
into a car-seat-bedroom, their children all knees and
buttocks and vibratory interstices as they glanced

off and on like a porch light with a necessary short in it
struck against eternity? The movie,
its embryonic miasma surrounding them like
jealous twins, allowed their sensing of the greater room
of universe, invited punching holes in make-believe
with patent-leather shoes sparking off car lights
as some drivers left for darker zones.

But to answer your question: I chose that cover,
no interloping editor. Its lovers glared up
out of their daring-dark by someone's camera snap
whilst kisses gouged black holes
into their heads and less distant galaxies. It had
something to do with a sepia photo
of my mother, head back, drinking a Coke while
leaning against a WWII tank, one leg extended flirtatiously
like a ramp to her private Berlin. Never having
seen her like that meant "the past" was orbiting
just out of reach, sloppily, like a moth testing the scald
of a light bulb. Who was she, anyway?
Someone not wishing to be ravished, but showing

that fringe of self-possessed delight, her high-heeled shoe also not
meant for ease in walking on any earth.

Did she dance all night?
Was the night also barefooted under its high-heeled
cave-ins? No silk like stockings making legs more skin.
We were lion-tamers then, women who squirmed
virginity back into its coin purse with the moon
slamming us on our backs. And as with these photos
I would tell you more if memory weren't a deflecting
of my pre-dawn hours where I rove in the dream-lush
against faces big as houses, and the gangsters
of the heart never run out of bullets.

(Response from Larry)

FIFTEEN LOVE, THE BLOOP-SHOT RETURN

I barely crack Tess's e-mail door,
her words and images thunder past
like Road Runner and Wile E. Coyote
zipping down a canyon.
I'm taken by a whirlwind twist,
like a Saturday morning cartoon tornado,
search for a salmon-net racket
to return what must be the fifteen-love ace shot—on
one knee I try a volleyball dig.

Slipstream vapor trails
vacuum me like a Hoover upright
going sixty on a tight-weave carpet,
riptides push flotsam.
Moses parts the Red Sea,
chance to catch the dervish of kisses
while her red babushka flaps,
cruising top-down on a zigzag street
after her slam.

I am a gangster in a double-breasted
suit with white wing-tip shoes,
I call her "Doll," this
horn-rimmed woman who loves
popcorn, especially old maids
she cracks like Wrigley's gum.

We crumple and fall into
each other. We are a half-eaten bag;
butter stains upholstery and each other
as if we were sixteen forever.

(Response from Tess)

A Dervish of Kisses

is served only when a dearth occurs
such as befell the wedding party in whose
invitation an "r" had been left out,
changing the prospects

entirely from dearth to death.
It was more than careless of
the printers, and of course nobody
came, at which time the band struck up
and the dancing inhabited us not
through the feet but smackingly
lip to lip as in those cartoons
where the lips suction the kissers

like toilet plungers, and when they part
each is propelled Frisbee-style into some
lost hotel of the mind where
they meet again as divorcées and have

a lot more fun cheating on their former
selves. He calls her "Doll-face," and
she calls him "Buster" and pushes
a rose bud into his double-breasted

lapel. It's a far cry from being out
to dinner these times in a one-horse town
and getting called "Baby Cakes"
by the waitress, which thing did actually
happen to me and, though meant to fatten
her tip, had the opposite effect. Meanwhile
Doll-face has smooched Chinese Red lipstick

onto his white neck-collar and Buster is
not worrying past the next foxtrot notion
of where this is heading, as the firmament
roils above them Van Gogh-style and they r
dancing r deathling into each other as darlings

without benefit of clegy yes *clegy*. Ah daling daling r'nt
she sweet? I ask you, r'nt she tweet?

(Response from Larry)

EVEN GANGSTERS NEED "R"s

"Adjectives are the pimples
of the English language."
—Nelson Bentley, Seattle poet

Like Vatican priests excommunicating
bad letters with a touch, a wedding invitation
without an "R" and the band plays
to grazing cattle and sheep.

Printers are mischievous gnomes
with clip-on ties and ink-streaked aprons,
who toil in two dimensions,
like kisses on a flat silver screen.

Without "R"s, what would
Baby Cakes call my black shirt
and white tie? Unceremoniously
I become Lay, transformed
from a proper noun into a verb,
not passive or present perfect.
I rejoice at not becoming a pimple.

Moll-doll knows the difference
between me, Lie and Lay.

On slick Naugahyde,
we conjugate verbs,
yogic-tantric vocabulary builders,
until flickers end, and candy-apple-red
Chevy Bel Airs and baby-blue
Ford Crown Victorias
sidle home under the orange August moon.

Between swaying arms of wheat,
I feel the hubcaps of my soul turning.
I yearn to glide across America's
neon heartland, visit every drive-in
before snow piles heavy
and only icy speakers hang
like the last sentinels of
midnight kisses.

(Response from Tess)

WHEN CARS WERE BEDROOMS

we did not worry our verbs over
vinyl seat covers in the dead-ends
of small-town streets, but luxuriated if
the wing-backed Buick's back seat was couch enough
for dreaming into each other, one of the pair tilted
on an elbow, gazing up into the kissing-moon
which always seemed to be shining those nights. What

happened to smooching? that edgy, pretend-it's-nothing art
of leading and leading past any culminating
action. For invitations did crave us. The blur of
stop signs would do. Or, maybe an opposite hunger,
our feet on virtual gas pedals as we sped across four-ways
and star-fall, train crossings and comet-sizzle
into the oncoming of dawn cow muzzles at
the windows, licking salt from the glassy day.

Thinking now of the 1929 Buick Master Six Sedan
Model 47 that could seat five passengers and boasted "full
vanity case equipment" (bumpers and spare tire
extra.) That gangster look, mob-comfort sheen. Remembering
Ray excited about his 1983 Turbo-Jet Mercedes, his wanting
there to be something especially for me, brightening over
its light-up mirror, its forehead hyphen of surreal doubling,
letting me put my eyebrows right. The boxy look
of its style come into fashion after his death, so strangers
interested in purchase leave cards tucked into
its windshield. A snowfall of calling cards
on the 1962 Buick Wildcat owned by a friend, touted
as the "new torrid luxury sports car" always speeding down
our minds in "stiff crosswinds. Pancake-flat cornering

on curves. Front bucket seats
divided by a console with tachometer and Turbine Drive
stick shift."

Tell me language doesn't
overwhelm the lay of any land! No wonder the word *hubcabs*
can tempt us into soul when we need to glide. Speech can be
more than wildcat, as Einstein knew, practicing
as a boy every sentence in a whisper before saying
it aloud, that difference between thought and saying
something intimate to another, the difference between lovers
on a speeding train kissing and the mere thought
of waving goodbye with nothing but a mind
whistling through the closed
interior of a sigh.

(Response from Larry)

WISP OF A GAL

Sun blazes on a September afternoon.
I perch cool in a pear tree
above zucchinis and cherry tomatoes,
study the world like a crouching ninja.

A vision appears:
aerodynamic fins, wrap-around windshield
and jet-aircraft grille on a '51 Buick Le Sabre
idling at a stoplight. Hubcaps spin,
my eyes whirl—kaleidoscope-colored chunks
slide, then twist until images click into focus. I see

Tess styling in a faux-fur coat
and Dr. Zhivago Russian winter hat
hiding a short bob. With perfect eyebrows,
thin and clean and eyeglasses dangling from a chain,
she chauffeurs me in Ray's gun-metal gray Mercedes
through downtown Port Angeles,
former bustling hub of boat builders with leather aprons
and wool-shirted lumberjacks. Town
weathered and shopworn by salty winds that
rise off the Straits of Juan de Fuca.

Her Irish brogue rolls like tapioca pearls,
mellifluous melodies and rhythms
that remind me of cigars and a squeeze box,
harmonica player who cradles Irish whiskey bottles,
stomps his boots on stage while rosy-cheeked women
bust a lusty river-dance jig on a warehouse floor.

I hear horses clopping as a wisp of a girl,
Tess, with long brown hair,
a young Lady Godiva in overalls, gallops
past the Deer Park drive-in theatre,
hive where she and her high-school
sweetheart smooch behind steamy windows
like a stack of pancakes hot off the griddle.

Cinema's hourglass queen of cleavage, lips and kisses
incinerates the big screen: Marilyn Monroe wiggles,
raises one leg at the knee, flipping her skirt up
with a high-heel kick, her gluteus is maximus,
like pears hostage under a tight red sheen,
twenty pounds of rice in a ten-pound bag.

I stretch for one more juicy treasure,
another sensual teardrop,
anticipate holding the pulsating oblong orb
of erotic and earthy fire overflowing
with so much ripeness that the tree
cannot hold it another instant.

Vertigo spins me upside down.
I am a teenage Icarus with aerodynamic fins,
wrap-around windshield, embracing the wind like
a young girl fluttering with billowing brown hair
away, away on horseback.

(Response from Tess)

EPONA MEETS X-MEN

Dressed as Epona for *LIFE MAGAZINE* in a long,
strapless sequined gown, I recline on a cushy borrowed horse
named Butterscotch. My elbow-length black
gloves and plumed eye-mask, purchased in New Orleans, tunnel
a mystery corridor back to first-century Rome. Celtic goddess,
protector of horses, donkeys and mules, astride a horse,
with her animals beside her, leaders of the soul in the afterlife.
Prior to the photo, I had just been thrown from
"Snow Heart," a horse named after my poem, when
the woman holding the bridle ducked her head out of the wind
to light a cigarette. Life is salted down

by inadvertent hinges where one motion triggers
another, like the simulated wind whirling up Marilyn Monroe's
skirt, ignited from a real moment of wind on 23rd Street
in New York City in 1901, borrowed from a short film
"depicting Florence Georgie walking over a grate, hot air
lifting her skirt." Camera clatter like a tommy gun
leading to 1955 and Marilyn's thigh-high echo
in *The Seven Year Itch*, still a kick into the future
with Kelly LeBrock, whose skirt wafts up in *The Woman
in Red*. I dust myself off from Snow Heart and wriggle
like a seal in a blanket onto Butterscotch like nothing happened,
resume goddess-lounge position encased
in silver sequins while Annie Leibowitz squares in
on me, snapping her mad-turtle lens like a drill-bit through

centuries. Marilyn's iconic ivory pleated dress at auction
selling for more than 5.6 million gives a wink to the one
on her statue at the Women's Museum in Dallas, skirt
whose flare has been captured pre-or-post-flare. Joe

DiMaggio, reported to hate the dress, smiles and lords it
over years of voyeurs, having been at leisure
with those thighs. Fashion carries skirts away
and gives us leggings so there is all the thigh one could want, but
sans the flesh, giving new meaning to "skin-tight." Comic
book heroine Jubilee revels in her Jackie Chan kick, unaware
of the real flesh-space between her high-top boots
and her snug blue shorts, shouting: "Eat your heart out!"

ZZZRRRK is the sound Storm makes when she leaps
her comic-book power-leap. With her we trade dizzy blonde
for steely white eye-sockets and snaking white hair, silver
body armor and curvaceous conical breasts rebounding light-clang.
Her lift-the-world shoulders mean she can handle it, would snigger
at a remark by my Irish visitor: "I was so happy I could have
snogged the face off him." No wind up Storm's skirt!
When she loses power and falls into the sea she rates a *SPLUSH*,
then crawls drenched to the nearest boulder to stare up defiantly
at the enormous Sentinel sent to yo-yo her back to captivity
on Genosha, a false utopia. Thrown

into THE BOX her last cry is *SKREEK!* Not HEEEEERE!
Jubilee, her mutant sidekick, plasma-blasts
a wire to pick her cell lock.
All routine for kidnapped mutants on holiday.

GIMME A BREAK! Jubilee cries as I shower them with sequins,
gallop past Marilyn and plunge into the spirit world
on Butterscotch.

19

(Response from Larry)

Starlings—

Before Jackie Chan is the prince
of chop-socky, we rope Bruce Lee,
(master of lightning attacks—
tear-your-nose-off-with-two-fingers or pop-your-eye-out
fanatic) into a game of pinochle at the UW cafeteria.
He plays without heart, mentally on his knees.
Mock combat drains his *chi*.

I recall a party at his studio on the Ave.,
Hong Kong Cha Cha champ is quiet,
rock music plays and three Everlast punching
and speed bags dangle.
At a glance they look like abandoned dance partners,
drooping, shopworn with no Celtic gods to protect them
unless Epona has pity on leather goods
along with donkeys and horses with
chestnut-sized eyes. At the Island County state fair I stare
deeply into equine windows and find
horses bite fingers poking through the mesh.
In spite of grand names—
Valkyrie and King, with golden trophies and blue ribbons,
they dwell amid dung piles with flies in eyes.

Unlike Tess with a Mardi Gras mask and her Butterscotch,
I once witnessed a vision galloping straight from
the *Conan the Barbarian* comic book sans thunder
and lightning, one of the four horsemen rampaging.
Magnificent Artemis, Greek warrior-goddess
in black leather boots and body armor with a breastplate
and swirls, raises a standard dangling fierce human scalps.
Ululating, her eyes flame atop a stallion

as large as the Trojan horse
with a magnificent curved neck, Clydesdale hooves,
and nostrils blasting steam, beast spawned from hell.

Villagers in a two-dimensional comic-book world
will turn their eyes to a red August sky
when Tess's curious three-dimensional face emerges
in their X-Man world, a round speck appears,
grows into an oblong nose. Puckered lips manifest below
until both features merge as one oval, then
shrink like an iris closing. Philosophers and soothsayers
will ponder the meaning, stir ashes
and examine tea leaves for hints about
the three apocalyptic mysteries witnessed
in two dimensions.

In a feeding frenzy starlings shriek and strip my fig tree,
black oily birds perch on the wire—hooded anarchists
dive and riot in the treetops pecking plump orbs.
I yearn to bake 50 in a pie instead of vainly throwing
tennis balls and dirt clumps.
Like the Luftwaffe they blitzkrieg in waves
bombing and strafing my precious London.

I will not crawl into a bomb shelter
but shake my fist like Churchill, cigar in hand,
and tie reflective ribbons that tinkle,
dangle and flash—things most birds dislike,
except, it turns out, starlings.

Agent Starling, Jody Foster in *Silence of the Lambs*,
her namesakes sporting pointy beaks, beady eyes
and unglamorous dark suits—everything except the lisp.
Would Hannibal Lecter savor them
with a little Chianti and fava beans?
Comforted in newspaper wrappings, I fortify figs, staple,
duct tape, and clip corners creating "strange fruit" under attack
on the tree, a merry-go-round without
cotton candy, full of paper nests
next to a cattywhumpus scarecrow.

After the Civil War ends, murdered black men twist
in Southern trees like clothes bags, Billie Holiday's song
protesting the "strange fruit" of their sacrificial lives.

Starlings, those battalions of shameless pillagers,
avoid my garden like Missouri homesteaders
stumbling upon an Indian graveyard. They
feel my savage gaze.

I mark my turf like a wild-eyed barbarian,
itch to scrape away civilization's veneer and ponder
dead starlings with "X"s in their eyes,
designs cartoonists bestow on the dearly departed.

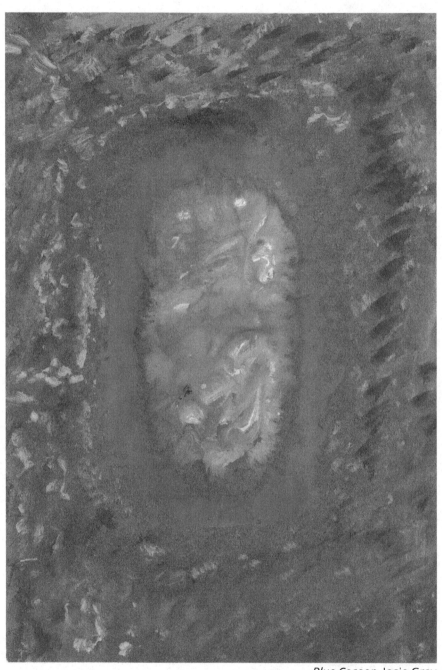

Blue Cocoon, Josie Gray

BLUE COCOON
Section II—Summer of 2015

Some thoughts from the poets
regarding *Blue Cocoon*

Blue Cocoon is the shortest of the three sections, and completed last, in the summer of 2015. Rather than place it in chronological order, the authors elected to locate it in the middle since *Wild-Haired Labyrinth Renga*, the second collaboration, supplied a more natural and fitting conclusion.

In *Blue Cocoon*, we consciously retained and promoted the spirit, energy and quirkiness from *Pow! Pow! Shalazam*.

Summer 2015

(Challenge from Larry to Tess)

ROSE CITY VACATION

In Ballindoon, lambing over
and hay baled high,
Josie wears his red shirt
as he drives to your County Sligo cottage.
After 40 years some call you *Yank* or *blow-in*,
woman with perfect eyebrows,
who attracts goldfinches, coal tits, and chaffinches
to a pastoral scene overflowing with bird calls and sheep
like marble headstones on the green fields.
Hedge cats skulk like Serengeti lions, nose

your rain-filled dish in anticipation. The two Eileens up the road
brew pots of Lyons or Barry's tea, expect you at their door
before Josie's family reunion where you claim your place
among his clan: sons, daughters, grandchildren,
great-grandchildren,
and his late wife's memory.

In Portland, Oregon I rise in my hotel room,
pillows strewn helter-skelter,
scene reminiscent of marshmallows floating
in a hell's broth. I recall our mutual friend, Alfredo,
who lands in Portland like a shanghaied sailor
unable to remember anything beyond
his Blue Moon Tavern binge in Seattle the night before.
Alfredo's adventure rivals the night he stacked

two unsecured paintings on the roof of his car,
navigated hills under the influence
and pinballed down Ravenna Avenue.
His canvases must have sprouted Edvard Munch-like

expressionist arms and hands to grip their extraterrestrial
mosaic faces in fear as they screamed all the way home.

I discover Portland is a carnival wonderland where
bacon drapes maple bars and pretzels impale chocolate
voodoo-doll donuts oozing raspberry blood.
Food-cart shantytowns sprout in downtown parking lots,

gypsy chuck-wagon villages, magnet for hordes of lip-smacking,
khaki-clad office workers and itinerant street musicians.
A visitor, I search for the *Yin* and *Yang*
of Portland's vibe, only to dodge
snares where amplitude sine waves intersect
and outstretched hands release grocery baskets piled
with bursting garbage bags.
Gauntlet of medieval palms reach out to me.

To the beggars, I am a lump of protein
zigzagging a trespass across *their* sidewalk,
sidestepping invisible webs that snag coins
in a spare-change geometrical world of angles.
Scrawled message dangles from a liberated Safeway cart,
The last person who stole this cart, owns it.

From my tenth-story hotel room,
I open curtains to a miniature crime scene below—
life-sized G.I. Joe action figure face-down—
twisted in a camouflage sleeping bag on the lip
of a vacant storefront.
No blood trails, blue police lights,
or crime tape—just a voyeuristic sense of peering

into private corners of a lost soul,
someone who in a different reality might have
killed enemies who looked like me.

In the morning I embark on an urban fishing adventure—
bind a net and two spinning rods,
pull a red Igloo Cooler strapped to a luggage cart
past food trailers and the Chinatown Gate
to the esplanade on the Willamette River's east bank.
My cart clack-clacks, echoes
through cardboard shanties in rhythm
with tires whining on bridge grates above.
Below the Burnside Street overpass,

glowing eyes track me like prey.
My designer glasses or yellow skin mean nothing here,
only the sound of rattling wheels—passport
to polite nods of recognition as if I were
a lost brother seeking the cathedral built for myself.

Tess, when lambing is over and hay is
wrapped in plastic like giant jelly rolls
scattered across the shorn fields,
what rattles your wheels when Josie gathers
his clan around the evening hearth?

(Response from Tess)

CAT MOUNTAIN

Polish coal rattles into the grate, signals
the ozone layer over Ballindoon that the EU's tax
won't snuff carbon fumes here any time
soon. Poverty, the great instructor, inhibits
change. Though overnight the Irish quit smoking
in pubs, they huddle to their open coal fires and will not
easily surrender them, even against taxes. These

are a people who ate grass during The Famine
to stay alive, and the old Chinese proverb says
"if a person can chew roots they will be able
for anything." I am among a people, Larry, able
for anything. I remind myself of this daily, watching
Mickey Moran head to the bog on his tractor
to haul out sticks to extend his coal fire. As for

shopping carts, it takes a 2€ piece to free one from
a locked chain of trolleys. Failing that, you must shop small
with a handbasket. Make trips. Poverty puts good legs
on some. Helmeted bicyclists whizz past my windows as petrol
goes up. The moon couldn't care less how we get around,

but I swear sleeping under the Sligo moon has swept my usual
dream-cargo free and cleared my spirit-realm of
festering. Like sleeping under cherry blossoms,
a gentleness falls through me, sifts my proclivities
for connecting to the troubles of others, and stays
temporarily my need to bind up the world's

miseries. Not to say I can't be outraged
by daily ignorance: the Sligo doctor quoted as

saying he could not tell if his East Indian patient had jaundice
"because of her color." At one report she has kidney failure,
the next she's dying: Dhara whom her husband called:
"*the light of my life.*" That light snuffed a few days after
her boy was delivered by caesarean. The inquest finds

her relegated to a maternity ward instead of ICU,
though she presented with "more than two organs in
failure." Bloods drawn, but not read. Doctors in attendance
but no alarms to save her. The worried husband mollified
by a nurse, told to get his wife a lemonade if he wanted to help
her. Here, Larry, skin color is more than punitive
with daily humiliations; it can cost you your life.

The headline actually read: "*We can't tell if Dhara has
jaundice due to Indian skin.*" I want to howl and crawl
into a hedge. I want to live on Cat Mountain, far from
such goings-on. Though months have passed since I left
for America, Bashō-cat has magically returned, perhaps
from Cat Mountain. I swear he raised a paw in a salute
of good luck, as I put down his dish of egg and fish.

I am worse than itinerant, more like a strange comet
that not only falls out of the sky but up
from the ground! Not even a cat should depend
on me. Especially since I fell while gathering lake stones
for the garden and broke my wrist. The Japanese warning
not to move stones by daylight
comes back to me. I hug the roadway hedge
to Eileen Frazer's only to find she's in Sligo General

with a broken hip. Ahh, we are such eggshell manifestations,
such feverish migrations. It's a wonder birds don't
entirely desert us, we who infuse the day with spiritually illiterate
peckings and preenings. Only my great-granddaughter Jade
saves prospect. She paints a bracelet of flowers
and cats' whiskers around my cast. The world needs more

of her. She can recite poetry and draw dogs
leading people around on collars to "Obedience School."
On my cast I wear to the NY premiere
of *BIRDMAN* she scribbles "Mummy Teresa," gets the giggles,
then cartwheels into the hydrangea. Oregon,
she says, is where you get "onto The Trail." She's
not sure if she would like "The Trail" but without it, she says,
nobody in America would have arrived anywhere
West. Most of all she'd like to meet an Indian. She'd trade

two magpie feathers for an eagle shaft, or
bargain black bogwood for a string of beads,
and be happy to go fishing with you, Larry. But you'd better
have something to trade. Remember she's of the tribe
that chews roots, a mighty lot. You'll recognize
each other, you being from the tribe
that forages mushrooms among
sword ferns. She says she would rather
go to Cat Mountain, though,
than to Oregon.

(Response from Larry)

CAT ISLAND AND BUNNY TOWN

While drift-fishing for king salmon at Point Defiance,
I spot a floater, not a plastic bottle or Coke can, but
a large black feather. Feathers should sink
among crabs and mud sharks, not
bob on green waves. Since there are no flying turkeys,
it must be from the bald eagle I call Icarus.

Like World War I biplane fighters, crows
dive for Icarus's tail feathers in flight,
harass and squawk, defending their turf.
I examine the feather closely. No UPC codes,
made in Japan, China, or USA markings.
It is a magnificent quill pen, something
Jefferson would have used to sign
the Declaration of Independence.

Your great-granddaughter, Jade, would have loved it,
except it is a federal crime to possess an eagle feather
unless you're a Native American. It carries
a $10,000 fine, amount that could free 4,000
Irish shopping carts from their 2-Euro cages,
depending on the currency exchange.

So I set the feather adrift with a short prayer
of thanks and good wishes. It swirls, then holds close
for a moment, like the bottlenose
porpoise who plays and follows me on occasion.
Gently the feather breaks free from my gravity
and floats like a happy wayfarer riding the currents
toward Vashon Island and Quartermaster Harbor
until it fades, a dot in the distance.

Tell Jade if I visit Ballindoon, I will take her
for a grocery cart ride past the pubs and stores in Boyle,
the nearest town. First I would liberate Josie's red shirt,
then don black and white war paint, tie a scarlet bandana
around her forehead and place a turkey feather in her auburn hair.
We would stop at every bakery, sweet shop and tearoom,
feast on delicacies—not grass or roots—
then trundle toward the horizon and disappear
like a movie iris dot near Eileen's cottage where

her teapot waits, cradled in a salmon-colored cozy.
I would tell stories about Tashirojima Island,
Japan, and how cats were shipped in to chase mice
that ravaged silkworm cocoons. When the company moved,
cats outnumbered villagers.
They had cared for the cats, hoping the felines
would bring good luck to the few remaining residents.

It was a scene reminiscent of the medieval maneki-neko story—
cat who raised its paw in salute as a rich priest's palanquin passed,
a sign the holy man should stop for the evening.
The poor village prospered when travelers learned
of the priest's favor, spawning hordes of ceramic
maneki-nekos and plastic charms to clutter Japan today.
Can you imagine an island governed by wily felines,

representing different independent parties?
You and Bashō, the hedge cat, would be in heaven
and I am sure the cat citizens would be
enlightened enough not to pass a coal tax.
Laws against dogs would serve better.

This village should not be confused with Okunshina, the island
of feral rabbits, which Jade would like more
than you and Bashō. Offspring of those used

for poison gas experiments run free
after the plant closed. Tame and friendly, they wander
the island protected. This twisted tale reminds me
of a movie-call for Japanese extras
I answered last week. They asked that I shave,
bring a white shirt and suit, only to stand around
8–10 hours for minimum wage. I declined
when I found the movie was about Japan winning

the war and occupying America.
That falseness meant my relatives in Hiroshima
and those in Nagasaki were never incinerated alive;
that the Japanese liberated us from American concentration
camps in the desert after 3 years of confinement; that we
would have been heroes, not the vanquished foe,

looking like the enemy after the war.
"Slightly jaundiced" would be the preferred national
skin color and all property lost from our unjust
incarceration would be returned. Ironically, this topsy-turvy
fantasy turned me inside out and badly disrupted
my psyche, unless, of course it was a comedy.
Alas, Tess, how many belly laughs can you
pack into a movie about America
losing the war?

(Response from Tess)

By the Sea

All afternoon in North Sligo lunching in the artist's studio:
tubes of paint, tubs of gesso, paintings
big enough to make your bed on. Sean McSweeney
and his wife Sheila dancing the conversation from rugby to
the Peace Rose planted early in their marriage, rose devoured
by sheep. Orna, their daughter, reads aloud,
Akhmatova in Russian, serves apple tart with full

cream, the apples picked dewy from the orchard.
I smile conspiratorially, pick up
my plate, rediscover the tongue,
that neglected snail. Cats have nothing
on us, Larry. We lick cream. Blessed freedom
to sit at table with one's grown friends in old age

and caress sweetness from a dessert plate.
The cats on Cat Island sit about all day licking only fur
while Chuang Tzu dreams he's a butterfly mistaken
for a bird. "Wake up! Wake up!"
we shout. "Wake up and be a man or
be eaten or mauled to death!" Chuang Tzu flutters open
his eyes and loses his life

as a butterfly. One less butterfly on Cat Island
makes no ripple on the indolence of cat multitudes
dreaming in sunshine. Meanwhile, the floating blue
at the center of Josie's painting has perplexed
Sean, who says "blue should always recede."
But this frisky, ill-mannered blue levitates
as *Blue Cocoon*, asking us to tolerate its daring

masquerade as art plundering the rules of art, blue
successfully deluding itself it doesn't have to lie down
to the artist's brush. Your refusal, Larry, to appear
in the movie slated to undo the outcome of WWII,
has kept mountains of history books from having to be
burned on street corners. Meanwhile Alejandro's *BIRDMAN*
pecks the indolent money-pocked eyes of the Hollywood

Buddha, trying to generate more than cookie-cutter
heroes. Josie's unruly blue raises its blue salute,
suggests we throw a party where we all lick
cream from white porcelain plates at a long table
by the sea—a blue-green sea that tosses waves
at Cat Island. When asked to offer a story, an Irish custom
at occasions, I'll tell of meeting the wizened man
near Lough Arrow who insisted I stroke
the breast feathers of his tethered falcon—after which
I quoted Wilfred Gibson:

> *Because I set no snare*
> *But leave them flying free*
> *All the birds of the air belong to me.*

Those lines, committed to memory, free
a multitude, our minds floating out like music.

If we provoke the imagination of the captor, even
for a moment, Larry, he might wake up from his
power-dream to witness
a leather glove of cow's hide flying from his empty hand
away, away over the blue-green fields.

39

(Response from Larry)

ISLAND WITHIN AN ISLAND

Chuang Tzu, dozing butterfly,
dreams of being a man.
Absent his vibrating wings,
the world spins sideways for a nanosecond.
During a harmonic convergence,
rain storms meant for parched vineyards
of the San Joaquin Valley twist through Port Angeles
and the Straits of Juan de Fuca.

Wake up, Chuang Tzu, your life is more than you think.

Like the sound of heavy cream slurped
from an apple-tart plate in Ballindoon,
smacking lips and gulping conjure squeeze-box
rhythms of an Irish ballad pulsating from Josie's brush,
spreading blue hues across the painting's heart.
I recall gazing down at Campbell Lake from

Mt. Erie on Fidalgo Island where an island sits
in a center of blue like a watercolor painting, an island
within an island. As the wind rises over the cliff, I remember
what my first and only wife used to say,
No man is an island, Larry, except for you.

Instead of quoting Gibson when asked to offer
up a story, I visualize a sugar-frosted Easter egg
topped with pink swirls, its clear plastic
viewing port with enclosed diorama of a miniature
bride and groom. I am the white-haired minister

in a blue aloha shirt next to the mossy waterfall
in Kubota Gardens. We stand on the cliff edge
under a canopy of pine trees. Anna's hummingbirds,
goldfinches and butterflies flutter in celebration. We are all
butterflies on the verge of morning.

Like an Irish sleepwalker, Josie wields his brushes,
madly paints Tess's Ballindoon cottage blue instead
of the promised white as she flies like an untethered falcon
over the Atlantic from Dublin.
Flap your butterfly wings, Chuang Tzu, parched
San Jaoquin hardpan and thirsty grapes beckon. Monarchs
cluster in the park, expect your entrance as the teapot whistles
a high-pitched warning.
Stop your nodding and chase sleep from

the silkworm cocoon of your mind, wake from lazy dreams
of hammocks and mulberry leaves. No longer
a sheltered worm, know you are
more than a Moon Pie treat, silent victim
of cat-lightning.

WILD-HAIRED-LABYRINTH RENGA
Section III—2013–2015

Wild-Haired Labyrinth Renga, Matt Matsuda

Some thoughts from the poets regarding *Wild-Haired-Labyrinth Renga*

Tess Gallagher, in the west of Ireland at her retreat cottage, and Larry Matsuda, in Seattle, exchanged nine interconnected poems during the summer, fall and winter of 2013 and through the winter and fall of 2014. Larry led off with "Careening Toward Forever-after," and Tess responded with "Dear Cloud, Dear Larry." As the exchanges progressed, Tess remarked that the process was similar to the *renga* where poets work from and respond to what the poet before has written. There is a syllabic structure too in a formal *renga*: one poet contributes three lines of seventeen syllables (5–7–5) and the other poet responds with a couplet of fourteen syllables (7–7) and the process continues in a repetitive fashion.

Since our original poems, though responsive to each other in free verse, did not comply with the *renga* form, it was decided we would title our work *Wild-Haired-Labyrinth Renga*. To satisfy the purist in us, we decided to add an actual *renga* as a thumbnail coda or snapshot at the end of each poem. But even the individual lines of the *renga* coda were written responsively by each of us.

For "Careening Toward Forever-after," Larry wrote three lines, and Tess returned with a couplet. Then Tess gave three lines for "Dear Cloud, Dear Larry," and Larry replied with a couplet until all poems had an accompanying 31-syllable *renga*. As a result, each long poem is followed by a similar thematic *renga*, somewhat like a wine reduction of the long poem.

Since the entire work contains numerous footnotes because it was conceived across cultures (Japanese American, Irish and Irish-American, Romanian, and East Indian) it is recommended that the work be read first in its entirety, then read again with the footnotes. Or one might simply like to read the poem first, then the footnotes, which is Tess's preference.

This piece connects seemingly disparate thoughts and moves by synaptic sparks that are both serious and playful.

Winter 2013

(Challenge from Larry to Tess)

CAREENING TOWARD FOREVER-AFTER

Car in reverse, I stomp the gas pedal.
Aluminum buckles, screeches like
a wounded brontosaurus.

My shrimp-fishing checklist for 5:00 AM:
license, lunch, and *life preserver.*
Open the garage door, not on the list.

So now what do we talk about when we talk about
crashing through garage doors?

Twisted rollers off track
hang cattywhumpus.
Dislodged metal sections dangle
a dismembered tin man, dancing.
Dorothy and Toto would drop
their jaws in disbelief.

If my antiquated cell phone
were capable, I would tweet
and text how to mangle
a garage door or I'd
post a photo on Facebook—
me flipping Luddite yellow pages
under a superimposed Eiffel Tower.

I muscle broken sections
like a Houdini weight-lifter.
Chevy exhaust pipe belches a cloud.
Metallic echoes still pinball my brain.
A crumpled door, wrecked accordion

gleams sunshine behind me.
On the water, fishing, my world is transformed
into a modern El Greco's *Storm over Toledo*—

Space Needle and Seattle skyline
to the East, snow covered Olympics to the West.
Riding Elliot Bay whitecaps I fantasize:
small prehistoric armored warriors
with prickly swords—shrimp as sushi: fried,
grilled, boiled, poached, and barbecued
Bubba Gump-style.

Tugging 400 feet of lead-weighted line,
water trickles from it like icicles melting.
Arms burn, shoulders ache,
and I wonder, *when will this torture end?*
As the trap surfaces, a caldron-boil of pink
spot-tailed shrimp hop, twist, and bubble
out of the cage like effervescent champagne.
I snap shrimp heads, peel translucent armor,
chomp crunchy tails.

As a child, my Buddhist Aunt Mitsumori
bribed me with a nickel to release
a spider from a Mason jar.

What would she say about panic-cries
from shrimp destined for a dip into wasabi
and soy, now drop-kicked into my Nirvana?
Did they bathe in a loving tunnel of white light

and meet a friendly face,
or encounter infinite fields of emptiness?

Under the sign of two fish facing each other,
I pass myself resting in deep pools
and discover a Moon Child, Tess,
Pacific Northwest Dungeness,
not a soft-shell crustacean[1].

Careening toward forever-after
and Grand Canyons of outer space,
Tess, what do you think
when you think about crashing
through garage doors?

*   *   *

> *Shrimp heads, asunder,*
> *float up like dismembered feet*
> *tight in orange Nikes.*
>
> *Even a wave goes walking*
> *on its one leg in fish feet.*

---

1 Tess Gallagher is born on July 21, 1943 under the sign of the crab: Cancer.

(Response from Tess)

Dear Cloud[1], Dear Larry,

As Mick Connaughton from up Barroe used to say—
'Ah ye's a right common idjit!' If only you'd been driving
a cart horse, Larry, your garage door would be safe.
In the villages of Romania where ruled Vlad the Impaler,
cart and horse cover all distances, but plum brandy[2]
puts drivers' heads wrong so they abuse these canny[3] little ponies.
Hearing this, I immediately signed over my heart to them
as they tossed along the roadways, their red
blinders zig-zagging with the swing of their heads, the whip

at the ready over their backs. Even off duty their harnesses
are left on them—something never done to our plough horses
in Missouri, and pasture to gypsies scarce so young boys are
stationed out in Dragasani[4] beside them in the tall roadside
grass. That would slow you down, Larry, on some hot afternoon
to take over for one of those boys, the cart horse
pulling grass and your mind climbing the green mountains
for mushrooms, as in your childhood. Gypsies took my friend
picking. They brought out a mess of them, which his wife cooked

---

1 *Dear Cloud* is just Tess's fond invention of a name for Larry to indicate his shape-shifting capabilities and how he can reflect light or become rain, can float above or inhabit. It is a kind of metaphor for his having multiple possibilities of drift.

2 *Țuică*: Plum brandy is called *țuică* in Romania and is the common celebratory drink to offer a guest or neighbor. There is a custom in Romania, when someone has died, of taking a drink of it and tossing the last of it to the floor or into the fire. In Hungary, the drink is known as *pálinka* and is often stronger; most Slavic countries call plum brandy *slivovitz*.

3 *Canny*: having or showing a practical cleverness or judgment: a *canny* card player, good at psyching out his opponents. Synonyms: *astute, clear-eyed, clear-sighted, hard-boiled, hardheaded, heady, knowing, savvy, sharp, sharp-witted, smart*.

4 *Dragashan* (English name) is a city in Vâlcea County, Romania, near the right bank of the Olt river.

with polenta for us—now there's trust—eating wild mushrooms
in Romania picked by gypsies! To squander ourselves
lightly, to be in mad company, to drink dazzling
white wine from a vineyard we walked through at dusk,
the village pickers' red and yellow shawls hung across
the row-starts above the roses, delicate sentinels planted

to warn of disease or insects attacking the vines. Instead,
there is list-making for exit or entrance—the most
tantalizing item on Ray's[5] last list: *Antarctica*, thrown in
with *cornflakes* and *spam*. Here in the west of Ireland
we are dipping sheep, feeding carrots to horses, planting
red peppers in a green jug, listening to the log-splitter

crack open the hundred-year-old beech that fell
across the avenue. Frazer's field, fresh cut, has yoked me
to my nose with sneezing. White roses in a bower[6]
at the window challenge my white newly painted cottage.
Today Josie cut wild jasmine at Kingsborough, mixed now
with mint, lavender and rhododendron in a vase. Reading Bashō
by firelight I marvel at the poet's stamina at a renga party—him

with a bad stomach, drinking sake all night on his knees, setting
the pace for eighteen others. Like him I am apprenticed
to clouds, which move about carrying everything they
need. Never mind my luggage held over in Paris with bottles
of Romanian wine for ballast. The wine came home unopened.

---

5 *Ray's*: Raymond Carver, Tess's husband who died at 50 on August 2, 1988, and
was called America's Chekhov for his world-renowned short stories.
6 *Bower*: a shelter (as in a garden) made with tree boughs or vines or, as in this case,
roses twined together in an arbor.

Dear Cloud, let's carry all we need and don't need too!
listing in our 14-ft. dinghy all the way to Malin Head[7]. I spent,
god knows, many the day as a child bailing my father's leaky boat

with a rusted red Folgers coffee can. If your garage door or
tail pipe is listing, at least you're only at sea in your mind, like
those on the hunt for romance or a good marriage match
in Lisdoonvarna[8] of a September eve, ten thousand swelling
the village streets—again, right common idjits! Still, I too
would give a euro or three to get that spider out of a jar in
your childhood. Dear Cloud, it's Ireland here and raining on
spiders and children playing in the graveyard. Let's float over to
the Arigna mines[9] where a man I met worked 29 years

on his side mining coal veins on a slant. Now he lists when he
walks and spits into a bucket. But his eyes—fierce enough
to bore their way to Rathland Island where the Campbells
tossed islanders to their deaths from the cliffs. He is sanguine
on his ventilator, smiles wanly as the doctor lights him a fag. Dark

---

7 *Malin Head* (Irish: Cionn Mhálanna) is located on the Inishowen Peninsula,
County Donegal, and is the most northerly point of the island of Ireland.
8 *Lisdoonvarna*: a village in County Clare where each year a matchmaking festival
is held, usually from August 31 to October 7. The center of this festival is dancing
but it has developed to one of the largest singles activities in Europe. "People don't
necessarily come to look for a spouse—they come by the thousands in search of a
good time." Originally the village was a spa town where visitors came to use the
mineral waters as a cure. Its name comes from the Irish to indicate the enclosure of
the fort in the gap.
9 *Arigna mines*: These coal mines, located in Derreenavoggy, Arigna, Carrick-On-
Shannon, Co. Roscommon, Ireland, were in operation from the 1700's until their
closure in 1990. Tours now show what it was like to work in some of the narrowest
coal seams in the Western world.

air—he knows the hollow taste of it—his head with all the light
    squeezed
out is another kind of cloud or spider-jar or human cry as
the gelatin ignites and a chasm opens a vein he can chip at. What

he feared, he said, was mice dislodging the fuse so detonation
timing couldn't be gauged. Yet mice, like roses to a vineyard,
could give warning—*no mice* meant an unsafe tunnel.
I'll clear out now, like mice floating through a miner's
dream. Josie[10] is singing *"her hair tied up in a black velvet
band,"* and twisting the lid on my spider's jar.

*   *   *

Cloud anatomy
and Bashō drinking sake,
spider-mind afloat.

Clouds devour pink lung lining.
Mice scatter helter-skelter.

---

10 *Josie Gray*: Irish storyteller (*Barnacle Soup & Other Stories from the West of Ireland*)
and painter, companion of Tess Gallagher's from County Sligo, Ireland for the past
24 years. See josiegray.com to view his paintings and to see a movie about how he
became a painter. The film contains images of Tess Gallagher's cottage and images of
her neighing to Josie's horses to call them up.

(Response from Larry)

OLD MICK'S WISDOM

Airstream-trailer-shaped clouds that resemble your
glowing white Irish cottage float by.
Unlike Eskimos and their 100 words for "snow,"
in Seattle we have one word for "rain"
often paired with a thousand adjectives
including "horizontal" which incidentally describes
what fell like a torrent of garage doors
and flooded my Japanese maple planter in an instant.
Fearing the tree would drown like spiders in a jar,
and assuming the dead-pony position, I tip it sideways.
Thick brown fluid tinged with musk and earth oozes.

In Idaho, puffy cotton balls float like
the Macy's Thanksgiving parade's Marshmallow Man
tethered above basalt canyons and gorges
that Evel Knievel jumps with his red-white-
and-blue motorcycle. Same black hole
tourists hungrily bungee into, an obliterating
plunge reminiscent of Dorothy's Kansas farm house
spiraling madly down to Oz. Idahoans call it Magic Valley,
formerly a desert, now endless fields of potatoes
and ten thousand Black Angus cattle
who de-gas and expel manure
a mile downwind from the former Minidoka Idaho
World War II Relocation Center[1], place I was born,

---

1 *Relocation Centers*: In 1942 approximately 120,000 Japanese American citizens
and Japanese nationals, without due process or the commission of any crime, were
incarcerated in American concentration camps called "relocation centers" by the
American government. Minidoka was one of the ten camps and at its peak housed
approximately 10,000 prisoners. The camps closed in 1945.

temporary home of 10,000 Japanese
corralled in the desert like stray cats.

Nearly sixty-eight years since Minidoka
was shuttered, my Japanese American artist friend,
Roger Shimomura from Lawrence, Kansas,
and I return to Minidoka for a symposium,
sneak out at break to scour Twin Falls antique shops
in search of the fabled porcelain karate-champ statue
that separates at the waist to become a sake container,
kitsch Bashō would have hated
even in his most inebriated state.

Back at the conference, they debate whether Minidoka
was a "concentration camp" or "relocation center."
Discussion swirls—I steal the microphone,
what do you call a prison in the desert with guard towers,
machine guns pointed in, armed guards, search lights,
barbed wire and soldiers who could shoot you if you tried to escape?
Not a "Dirty Dancing" summer camp in the Catskills!

Afterward Roger honors me with lapel buttons he created,
Minidoka Croix de Guerre trifecta:
Born in America; *I am not Chinese*; and *I speak English*—
reminders he thinks useful for travels in white America.

Our conversation slides from the sublime
to airstream-trailer-shaped clouds that resemble your
glowing white Irish cottage, then on to colonoscopies,
procedures we both experienced. We marvel
at how over five feet of scoping leads to enlightenment.

Then agree colonoscopies be administered
to every politician and bureaucrat so that
Romanian wine does not become ballast,
off-duty cart ponies are un-harnessed,
and garage doors hang safely like glassed-in spiders.

I recall Josie's story about his country cousin
who once thought to blast cobwebs
from his barn with dynamite, successful at first until he
enthusiastically blows up the entire barn.
Did I say "barn"? Or maybe it was "brain"—
like your coal-miner friend whose dynamite, you say,
"ignites a chasm and opens a vein he can chip at."

Oh what would Mick Connaughton from up Barroe
say about exploding barn doors, airborne spiders
and mice munching dynamite fuses
in silver Airstreams of the mind?

*   *   *

Nisei rip electric
barbed-wire fences in protest,
cattle status rejected.

When an act is inhumane
it echoes past excuses.

(Response from Tess)

Button, Button

for Lawrence Matsuda

I

Green Peach[1], that's the button Bashō asked Roger
Shimomura for when he saw the "I Am Not Chinese" button
Roger gave to Larry Matsuda as a gift at the Minidoka reunion.
But, at the Irish renga party in Stokestown following
the opening of the new wing of the Famine Museum[2],
a smart-aleck thought Bashō's terse pen name
had insulted *Greenpeace* and gave him

a shiner. Indeed, *Green Peach*, the recalcitrant
pith of it, was an unlikely name for a poet. As for me,
in Ireland I need a button proclaiming me *Not a Banker*,
where honest folk lose homes daily and nationalized banks
send a country into debt while their managers join arms in a jig
singing "Deutschland Uber Alles!"[3] Thank the Berkeley antique

---

1 *Green Peach*: the first pseudonym Bashō, famous Japanese haiku and tanka master, took for his writing.

2 The Famine Museum at Strokestown Park, Strokestown, Co. Roscommon, Ireland, is located in the original Stable Yards of Strokestown Park House. It was designed to commemorate the history of the famine of Ireland and in some way to balance the history of the "Big House." The Great Irish famine of the 1840s is now regarded as the single greatest social disaster of 19th-century Europe. Between 1845 and 1850, when blight devastated the potato crop, in excess of two million people—almost one-quarter of the entire population—either died or emigrated.

3 *"Deutschland Uber Alles"*: The National Anthem of Germany, composed by Joseph Haydn. This reference recalls the Anglo Irish Bank's former manager's singing "Deutscheland Uber Alles" in a taped telephone conversation with former chief executive David Drumm. The managers knew that the billion-euro aid package from the European Union would not be enough. That's why they swore about naive German savers who would have to foot the bill ... before singing gleefully the first verse of the song "Deutschland Uber Alles."

emporium sincerely, Larry, for the 1960s *ABORTION NOW*
button, though I could not wear it with impunity

to the Strandhill Ballroom of Romance, even having
re-adjusted the baby-bump pillow in my trousers when
I glimpsed the priest and ducked
into the Ladies. There, a 14-year-old held out
a crisp bag[4], collecting spare change to get to England
on the boat for her solution[5]. Cut marks in a ladder
on her wrist had failed to convince a judge her life was

in jeopardy, her attempts so "amateurish." "Ah, you'd
have to slice a jugular, and sure, what would be
the point? You'd bleed out then and there," she sighed
and thumped my pillow as if she'd like to take a nap.
I dropped her a 50-euro note and skint past her belly,

---

4 *Crisp bag*: potato-chip bag in Irish English. Here the reference is to the fact
that women cannot easily or safely gain access to abortion (rape and incest are
not reasons for abortion in Ireland); the usual route would be to cross to England,
usually on a boat. If they have no funds or support they have to collect that passage
and cost money somehow. Holding out a chip bag in a pub is my imagined ironic
emblem of the desperation of their plight.

5 *Limited Abortion law*: In Ireland the question of whether a woman threatening
suicide because she is pregnant would be allowed an abortion was brought forward
during the vote for the so-called "limited abortion law," which did pass on July 12,
2013. Under the restrictive legislation, one doctor will be required to sanction an
abortion in the case of a medical emergency; two in cases where there is a physical
threat to the life of the pregnant woman; and three—including either an obstetrician
or gynecologist and two psychiatrists—where there may be a risk of suicide.

on her neck a cameo of Savita[6] secured by a black

velvet band. Savita, our lady killed by a heartbeat.
Savita, who took her degree as a dentist in India, and
came to Ireland to die of sepsis and neglect in a Galway
hospital, an "untenable pregnancy" gone wrong in Catholic
Ireland, her care put aside for her child's vanishing
heartbeat. "Take my child," she'd pleaded earlier,

to no avail, as she traded her own heartbeat for her dying baby's
silence. *Savita, Savita* our lady of long-suffering,
who believed her death would not be required. I drop
my *not a banker* button into the crisp bag, and Savita smiles
shyly from the girl's neck, as if she knows her husband
is taking her death all the way to the Court of Human Rights.

---

6 *Savita Halappanavar*: an immigrant from India to Ireland, who died in University
Hospital, Galway, on 28th October, 2012, from multiple failures in treatment, but
also because confusion over the anti-abortion law became a "material factor." She
had been hospitalized with an "untenable pregnancy." However, under Irish law at
the time, the life of an unborn fetus was to be put before the life of the mother.
The baby's heartbeat had to stop before it could be removed from her womb. Savita
Halappanavar subsequently died of sepsis due to inattentiveness to her own care
during this doomed pregnancy. There were worldwide protests in India, Great
Britain and in Ireland. A full inquiry found that she had died as a result of what was
ironically called "medical misadventure." Her death became the stimulating factor
in reconsideration of the affect of the anti-abortion law in Ireland, which *prohibits
abortion even in cases of rape or incest*. Those issues remain the same, but a new law
passed on July 12, 2013, gives better consideration to the fate of mothers when
their lives are at risk in childbirth.

59

II

The moon is so bloated I think its mirror-moon
in Lough Arrow will pull it down. Let me wear the button
stamped *Moonbeam* all the way to the bottom.

Bashō has written in my dream: "*See you at Sun Ya Bar*[7]."
That "dirty vodka martini" I had with you there, Larry, at our
between-planes feast still beckons. But when, oh when!
will Roger inhabit the dark corner in the bar with a solitary
Scotch so our glances can meet? I promise to engineer
an appearance *if* Kansas blows him our way. I could give him

some of my signature "portable kisses," red as a goldfinch's
beak-rim, for his next painting. Irish Red, let's call it,
though these finches migrate from Africa. Birds
have no boundaries and so, dear Cloud,

---

7 *The Sun Ya Bar*: famous bar located in the Seattle International District and
formerly attached to the Sun Ya Restaurant now the remodeled annex to the Ocean
Star restaurant. Roger Shimomura, famous Japanese American painter, frequents
it and also occasionally other poets, writers and artists such as Lawrence and
Karen Matsuda, Tess Gallagher. "*At 4 on a Tuesday afternoon, the bar is half-full but
pregnant with promise. Every patron is on the wrong side of 40, with blacks and whites
peppered (or salted) among a mostly Asian crowd. Three television sets of varying sizes
show Hurricane Isaac hitting Louisiana, Asian art adorns the walls, and red paper bulbs
hang from the black tile ceiling, muting the lights. Against the back wall rest a wood
stove and dartboard, both out of commission, and swivel chairs make for a potentially
great bout of bumper drunks. The Bartender: tall, dark-haired Gloria Ohashi boasts
a deep voice and quick wit. 'We don't have regulars,' says Ohashi. 'We have lifers.'*"
Reviewed for *Seattle Weekly*, Sept. 11, 2011, by Mike Seeley.
In June of 2015, the Sun Ya Restaurant and bar were remodeled and changed
owners. Fortunately, the bar's character remains much the same in spite of the
physical upgrades.

they don't agree to confinements, nor passports, nor
gun turrets, nor dispossessions, nor calling what was done to
Japanese American citizens during WWII anything but words
reserved for the worst injuries to spirit, body, and mind.
Maybe though, along with a concept like "concentration camp"
to recalibrate the level of harm, we need more tellings, more stories
with exact details of what was suffered.
Nothing substitutes for that.
Josie is humming the opening bars of "*There was an auld woman*

from Wexford, in Wexford she did dwell. She loved
her husband dearly, but another man twice as well.
With yah rum dum dum dum dee-ro
and the blind man he could see!"[8]

Which song ends in a bad way for the auld lady,
so I shall turn in my moonbeam for a javelin and cinch up
my babushka for certain travail.

*   *   *

> *Moonbeam, we need your*
> *accusing light: Our Lady*
> *Savita has died.*
>
> *Slow death by bureaucracy:*
> *civilized, remorseless.*

---

8 "*The Old Woman From Wexford*" (also known as "Eggs and Marrowbones") is a
traditional folk song which, like so many old folk songs, has origins lost to history.
It's a humorous ballad, wherein an unfaithful old woman is taught a lesson when
her blind husband steps aside and she plunges into the lake, instead of her designed
intent of pushing *him* in!

Tess Gallagher & Lawrence Matsuda

(Response from Larry)

HOLY FIG

Without borders, your goldfinches
migrate like my *Ficus regina* fig tree.
Undisciplined green Godzilla rises
above telephone wires and exports wild branches
over the neighbor's white picket fence,
proliferation of celebratory leaves,
sentinels that could guard the modesty
of 100 Adams and Eves full of their apple-
induced knowledge of good and evil.

Pope Paul IV vaccinates impure thoughts
with aprons, fig leaves and jock straps
over marble statue genitals,
gesture that reminds me of my US army stint.
Government inoculates troops against:
typhoid, paratyphoid, polio, smallpox,
black plague, but lets us catch meningitis.

I snip fig tree shoots and yank out
branches burrowing in the dirt.
Spider-like roots encroach
into my raised tomato bed.
I twist and turn tangles of fig boughs
toward the trunk. I handcuff limbs
and recall the sweet-faced 14-year-old girl,
pregnant, with an empty crisp bag, gasping
for a solution outside Ireland.

Tess, as the phrase goes,
You gave a fig about her
or maybe 50, amount Buddha would

have dropped if he traded in Euros.

I too know empty crisp bags.
As a child I peer into my father's cloudy eyes,
He rests in bed with a bleeding ulcer,
nothing beyond the clouds—
when he can't stand and falls down at work,
nothing beyond the clouds—
when depression takes Mom away,
nothing beyond the clouds
except years of empty crisp bags
and hopes of finding a solution.

Under the shade of a sacred fig tree,
Siddhartha meditates 49 days.
Enlightenment flows like sap,
thunderbolt that bypasses Irish doctors
over 2,000 years later.
A bullet, spear point or arrowhead would have

clanked in a metal surgical bowl,
but Savita, born in the land of Siddhartha,
dies as doctors walk away from an untenable fetus
whose heartbeat outlasted hers.

How their physician consciences must ache
knowing they and their oaths are shams,
bolstered by misbegotten mandates.

Savita's husband and family mourn
her senseless martyrdom, carry the indelible

weight with scars across their hearts,
face nothingness that remains
beyond the clouds.

Before her spirit touches Nirvana,
did doctors say, *I couldn't give a fig,*
abusive remark that dates back to Shakespeare,
an obscenity that stains
like Savita's outrageous death,
a bleeding ulcer on the breast of Ireland
a thousand fig leaves could never cover.

In this medieval forest,
where is the sunbeam from heaven
and the righteous button slogan, *Remember Savita,*
that begets a solution?

*   *   *

> *Modern holy wars,*
> *righteous deaths, aerial*
> *lightning from drone strikes.*
>
> *Scattershot oblivion*
> *rains down on the innocent.*

(Response from Tess)

THE PAPER AIRPLANE OF JUSTICE

On Caroline Street the seven-year-old boy
across the fence floats his paper airplane over
to me. At eight I must seem exotic.
One lands in my hair and lodges between my
pigtails, which to the airplane launcher could be
Mozambique. I'd heard a lot about Justice
since my father belonged to a union
and I knew the Airplane of Justice (name
scrawled in my mind on the airplane's inward reaches)
did not belong in a girl's hair. Naturally I reached

up and freed it, then tried to wing it back to him.
But Justice being unwieldy, it veered off into the dahlias
to be immediately commandeered by earwigs. They
must have thought it handy indeed with its pristine
streamlined folds and pointed fuselage sans
propellers. Justice in the 1950s was rudimentary,
only a matter of getting the folds right. Unfazed,
I knew my duty and retrieved the plane and its cargo
of hysterical antennae, then zinged it back to the boy—
Edward, I think he said his name was. This time it took

air and soared until it nose-dived miserably to his feet
and turned upside down, the earwigs having braved all this,
now considering themselves its crew. The boy, Edward,
like an Englishman I would meet much later in life,
wanly smiled and, in a mysterious show of bravery, smattered
the earwigs on the sidewalk. Justice often took no hostages, or
if it took them, did so on trains in broad daylight,
allowing its participants one suitcase each, as happened to
your parents, Larry, sent into the Idaho desert. Edward and I

could have stayed like that for days, for years—buoyantly,

precariously floating the Airplane of Justice back and forth
across a picket fence, except that it began to rain. We took
little notice until the soggy paper splayed open to its creased
center fold. Edward stroked his fingers again and again over
the faint imprint of the Engine of Justice to no avail. It
sputtered rain and grime from his dirty finger tips. No,
flight was out of the question. It was then I managed to
flutter lightly over the fence in my flour-sack dress sewn by my
grandmother in Missouri, and together Edward and I

performed an impromptu rain-dance burial right there,
in Edward's front yard, strewing dahlia petals and
pansies like crippled butterflies over the collapsed remains
in respect for all the effort at flight its paper had made
that long-ago afternoon. I recalled today the simplicity,
delight and matter-of-fact acceptance at the crumpled
outcome of our serious play. Edward grew up to be a coroner
in a tidy Eastern Washington town, whilst I came to Ireland
to write poems and live in a cottage by a lake near

an ivy-covered abbey. Daily I read *The Irish Independent*
where Savita, dead of "medical misadventure,"
as the examining committee determined, became
the victim of her unborn baby. Now with Savita's memory
to propel him onward, her father in India announces
he will sue the Galway Hospital.
'No more women in Ireland must die as she died,' he says,
though he knows suing won't bring her back—Savita
with the vermillion bindi, her smile like white diamonds

beaming in life all over Ireland in the paper Airplane of Justice
in *The Irish Independent*. How frustrating

Irish weather must be to young boys and girls
floating their paper airplanes, I think, as I fold this poem
into its hopeful winged shape, lift it to soar above Jimmy
Frazer's field toward America, where in another form,
you, Larry, will click it up unhindered by rain and struggles
with the intricate water-seeking root system of your fig tree
from which I must beg some cuttings.

*   *   *

Justice, my paper
airplane, delivers earwigs
from the dahlias.

First-class shadow-passenger—
injustice demands its due.

(Response from Larry)

GHOST DAHLIAS

Justice is a paper airplane
fragile in its twisting flights
and break-nose landings,
design not meant to defy gravity for long.
In the instant before paper strikes rock,
mother earth claims victory. Those
entitled are served justice like *soupe du jour*,
innocent late-risers routinely

crushed like earwigs after the fall.
Falsely we believe all deserve the fruits
of flight, as if our names are Wallenda,
leotard-clad bodies forever cartwheeling
without nets[1]. As an eight-year-old,
you stand alone by the white picket fence
on Caroline Street in Port Angeles.

What a sight—frayed pigtails
held tight by red rubber bands taming
a wild splay of brown waves. Woven strands,
ideal for inkwell dipping and butterfly landings
as the west wind rises over the Straits of Juan de Fuca.
With outstretched arms you embrace each gust,

your homemade sack-cloth dress billows like a sail.
Proudly you sport red-striped knee-length socks
pulled over stork legs that poke out

---

1 *The Flying Wallendas*: circus performers for the Ringling Brothers Circus, from the 1930s, famous for the seven-person chair pyramid act on the high wire without a net. The "flying" label was earned when four members fell and survived relatively unscathed. In 1962 they fell again and two died.

of a pair of black bone-dry school-patrol
high-tops. Leather shoelaces crisscross and sprout
from copper-colored eyelets, and snug tight
to the hooks near the top of the tongue.

You are a young boy's vision of first love, part waif,
part rustic wonderment, facing Edward's
two-story house. Ruled by latitudes and longitudes
of earth's magnetic fields, momentarily your body
assumes a twisted pose reminiscent of Wyeth's painting
of Christina in a pink dress with dark hair. She crawls
crab-like in a field of dry grass, grasping
and stretching toward the house on the hill.

You tilt your head and stand frozen at the fence,
hold your breath for Edward to appear
and zing his paper glider.
His missiles mean to lasso your heart but
fall short, close enough like horseshoes
to lure you over the barrier
for an impromptu mud-and-dahlia dance.

Continuing the jig could have landed
you in a small Eastern Washington village,
wife of the town coroner, official who each day
touches those that gravity has overtaken.
He might have listed Savita's passing as
"an overdose of injustice resulting in death,"
an admonishment to people of differing ethnicity
who should know better than to attempt
a risky childbirth in Catholic Ireland.

That imagined marriage union between you
and Edward is light years from where you left
your boots in a heap to pose barefoot on a mare
named Butterscotch for Annie Leibovitz. In the photo,
your long hair glistens like a horse's mane, precious image
not unlike Whoopi Goldberg's face and limbs
peeking from a bathtub of milk, and Meryl Streep
pinching and pulling her white mime face
into a Kabuki actor's visage for a *Rolling Stone* cover.

You are Icarus's sister at undreamed heights.
With a 20-foot wingspan and rack of a 1,000 bald-eagle feathers,
you glide above green seas and blue hills
to warm hives and stone temples among distant stars that flicker,
place where paper airplanes go to die, beyond the pull of justice.
Air so thin only Fate, Karma and ghost dahlias reside.

*   *   *

> *Sack-cloth hunger pains,*
> *transform silk dreams into yachts*
> *and Mercedes Benz.*
>
> *Pack my bag like Rosco Gordon,*
> *blues man kicked from a fountain[2].*

---

2 Rosco Gordon: Famous Beale Street bluesman who as a child was kicked away
from a water fountain by a white man. When he died, his bags were packed for his
next gig.

(Response from Tess)

IF YOUR BROTHER'S WINGS ARE MELTING

one might hope for a sea beneath him, except
that, you guessed it, he can't swim: thus
he drowns and has to live on in the useful
form of a warning—that if your wings are
made of wax, make sure to wear a life preserver
over your wetsuit and do your flying only over
the Irish Sea where the sun is sure to have gone
elsewhere. Sadly, the lives of cats are similarly
instructive. I recall the demise of my first cat, Tiger Lil,
explained to me at the age of two as caused by her

having eaten too many snakes. I vowed then and there
never to eat snakes and have kept to that. One's survival
does seem fraught with advice, which, however well intended,
often fails, in its expression, to catch our attention. Why,
for instance, didn't Daedalus warn his son that if he
flew near the sun he'd simply end up as
"skinny-jeaned indie landfill," or swamp him with
"an inconvenient flow of parliamentary
language" if he proposed flinging himself from the nearest
castle tower or crumbling abbey: "Take a trial flutter

from yon bog stump, me lusty lad," is what Daedalus
should have said, "and let's see does this contraption
work." Or, the odd threat might have caught his son's fancy:
"if you fall you'll be considered nothing but a poor
misguided wannabe, and whatever is left of you will likely be
traded out to Hungarian sex traffickers as relics

for pagan rituals." Thank you, Brian Boyd[1],whose sashays
through the music scene in the *Irish Independent* prove
that, had Boyd been the father of Icarus, the boy
would likely have listened, then told his dad to take

his wax-winged affliction of comic inevitability and strap
it to his own backside and jump off the Giants' Causeway
at some high noon imported from an African heat wave.
But no, we get lost in what a good, obedient, trusting son
Icarus was to—yes, yes daddy—strap on that pair
of perishable would-be wings that even
a queen bee's laziest honey-drunk drone would have
recognized as a death-buoy. The successful
warnings of my own childhood usually began "If
you don't" followed shortly by endearments such as
"you'll wish you were an angel on a burning

Christmas tree in hell when I get finished with you!"
The sought-after Tiara of Fear meant to drip
its scalding candle-wax of obedience somehow never
seeped into my brain. I saw myself rather as a kind of
interplanetary octopus grabbing up alternatives
as fast as anything failed me. Of course
Daedalus did fly successfully off Crete with those same

un-microwavable wings, and for the myth's sake went on
to engineer temples and serve other kings. But now we

---

1 *Brian Boyd*: A columnist on music for *The Irish Independent*. This paper is generally
perceived as being politically liberal and progressive, as well as being center-right
on economic issues. (Wikipedia) Tess reads it every morning when she is in Ireland.

have stumbled into the labyrinth, one of his better inventions,
though the seven virgins devoured yearly by the Minotaur
might not agree, and I must return on their behalf to
my *Independent* to check out the disgruntled visage of
the Fine Gael Party Whip, Lucinda Creighton[2], who has been

dropped from the party for voting against
the "limited abortion bill" generated by Savita's death
in childbirth, Savita smiling diamonds as Lucinda
clears out her desk, scoops up her €40,000 severance pay
and clatters down the long Hallway of Justice, Savita
snacking on the Minotaur, pulling out the virgins one
by one from his gory maw by their hair, Savita urging us along
until we stumble into sunlight, tethered to an ant
who led us free, not knowing the way.

*   *   *

Savita impugns
her tormentors: limited
abortion rights gained.

White covers sweet coat-hanger
victim, sepsis odors swirl.

---

2 *Lucinda Creighton*: Party Whip who disagreed especially with the suicide
provision in the proposed and ultimately adopted "limited abortion law." When a
party whip goes against her party she cannot continue in that position and must be
dropped from the party. Having been dropped, she has been forming her own party.

(Response from Lawrence)

In Memory of Kip

Tess, the day I received your last poem
from Ireland about your brother's wings,
my friend, Kip, died of a heart attack while
casting trout lines on a small Whidbey Island lake.

Shocked and brain tired,
I consult your imagination
where Native American visions reside.

You instruct me to build a driftwood bonfire at midnight
on Alki beach, near the stone lighthouse on the Salish Sea
where silver salmon school in green kelp beds.
Orange flames explode gnarled limbs and branches
as they spark into crackling fireflies.
Smoke sprints north over the bay
like skywriter vapor trails, leaving charcoal
for war paint and petroglyph drawings.

You share a prayer with me,
Nam-Myoho-Renge-Kyo[1],
mystical Buddhist sutra of the Lotus
unfolding to enlightenment.

I strike the brass singing bowl.
Clear like a cast iron bell it rings. Then
crisp high pitch fades to a thin thread.
Echoes call bald eagles nesting
in cedars above the sandy cliffs.

---

1 *Nam-Myoho-Renge-Kyo*: Buddhist chant intended to awaken enlightenment and
the Buddha within.

Under a full moon,
above roiling whitecaps,
black and white messengers glide,
dive and summon the orca pods.

A fisherman king has died.

Acknowledgments

Pow! Pow! Shalazam appears in *Plume*, April 19, 2003.

"Kisses," "What They Missed," "Fifteen Love, the Bloop-Shot Return," "A Dervish of Kisses," "Even Gangsters Need "R"s," "When Cars Were Bedrooms," "Wisp of a Gal," "Epona Meets X-Men," "Starlings"

http://plumepoetry.com/2013/04/featured-selection-pow-pow-shalazam-by-lawrence-matsuda-and-tess-gallagher

"Wisp of a Gal," "Fifteen Love the Bloop Shot Return," "Careening Toward Forever-After" and "In Memory of Kip" appear in *Glimpses of a Forever Foreigner*, Lawrence Matsuda, CreateSpace, South Carolina, 2014

Wild-Haired-Labyrinth Renga appears in *Plume*, May 8, 2015.

"Careening Toward Forever-after," "Dear Cloud, Dear Larry," "Old Mick's Wisdom," "Button, Button," "Holy Fig," "The Paper Airplane of Justice," "Ghost Dahlias," "If your Brother's wings are melting," "In Memory of Kip"

http://plumepoetry.com/2015/03/featured-selection-12/

Art Credits

Cover Art: *Boogie Scribbles* by Matt Sasaki, mattsasaki.com

American verses American by Roger Shimomura, 54" x 54", acrylic, 2010, collection of the artist, rshim.com

Blue Cocoon by Josie Gray, 9" x 13", gouache, 2014, Bay Street Gallery, josiegray.com

Wild-Haired Renga by Matt Matsuda, 6.67 x 10, digital paint/photo/3D, 2015, mattmatsuda.com

Portrait: *Tess Gallagher: I Never Wanted to March* by Alfredo Arreguin, 30" x 24", oil on canvas, 2004, collection of Tess Gallagher, alfredoarreguin.com

Portrait: *Lawrence Matsuda* by Alfredo Arreguin, 30" x 24", oil on canvas, 2015, collection of Lawrence Matsuda, alfredoarreguin.com

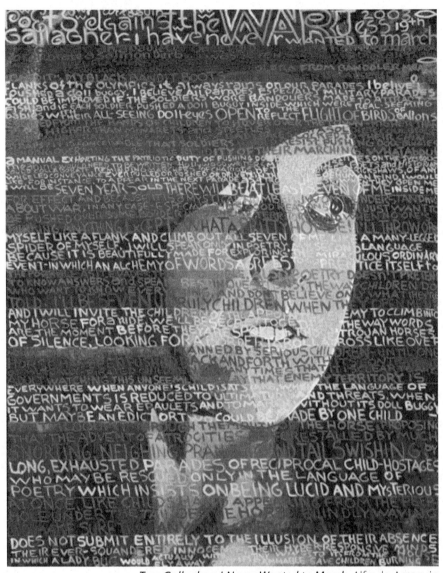

Tess Gallagher: I Never Wanted to March, Alfredo Arreguin

TESS GALLAGHER's latest book *Midnight Lantern: New and Selected Poems* (Graywolf), was published 27 September, 2011. Graywolf also published *Dear Ghosts* and *Moon Crossing Bridge*, as well as other works, including her selected stories, *The Man from Kinvara*. Her essay collections, *A Concert Of Tenses* and *Soul Barnacles*, are also available from University of Michigan Press. She recently companioned the film *BIRDMAN*, which includes one of the short stories of her late husband, Raymond Carver: "What We Talk About When We Talk About Love." She became an encourager of its director, Alejandro Inarritu, throughout work on the film, and their friendship led to his mentioning her as he received four Oscars for the film in 2015. This friendship continues through Inarritu's work on *The Revenant* during which Tess sent him poems he said he read to energize himself at breaks in the arduous filming process.

She wrote "a poet's introduction" to *Marina Tsvetaeva: The Essential Poems*, translated by Michael Naydan and Slava Yastremski, published in 2015.

She lives and writes in Port Angeles, Washington, her birthplace, as well as intervals spent in her cottage in the west of Ireland, where all of the poems included here were written in her chair that overlooks Lough Arrow and Jimmy Frazer's green field in County Sligo.

Lawrence Matsuda, Alfredo Arreguin

LAWRENCE MATSUDA was born in the Minidoka, Idaho, World War II Relocation Center, a concentration camp. He was among the approximately 120,000 Japanese Americans who were held without due process, some for three or more years. Matsuda has a Ph.D. in education and was a visiting professor at Seattle University. In 2005 he and two colleagues co-edited the book *Community and Difference: Teaching, Pluralism and Social Justice*, Peter Lang Publishing, New York. It won the 2006 National Association of Multicultural Education Phillip Chinn Book Award. In 2010 Black Lawrence Press published his first book of poetry, *A Cold Wind from Idaho*. "Minidoka Fences" also appeared in *Cerise Press* 1:3, Spring 2010.

His second book, *Glimpses of a Forever Foreigner*, was released in August of 2014. It is a collaboration between Matsuda and artist Roger Shimomura. In 2015 he completed two graphic novels with art work by Matt Sasaki and interviews with Japanese American fighters from the 442nd and their relatives; part one, *An American Hero: Shiro Kashino*, was released in April 2015 and part two, *Fighting for America: Nisei Soldiers*, was released in September 2015, published by Wing Luke Museum and Nisei Veterans Committee Foundation.

obtained

9 781941 196298